The WARMED HEART

The WARMED HEART

30 Days in the Company of John Wesley

MARK A. HARMON

Beacon Hill Press of Kansas City
Kansas City, Missouri

Copyright 1995
by Beacon Hill Press of Kansas City

ISBN 083-411-5557

Printed in the
United States of America

Cover design: Crandall Vail and Mike Walsh

Scripture quotations not otherwise designated are from the King James Version of the Bible.

Permission to quote from the following copyrighted version of the Bible is acknowledged with appreciation:

The *Holy Bible, New International Version*® (NIV®). Copyright © 1973, 1978, 1984 by International Bible Society. Used by permission of Zondervan Publishing House. All rights reserved.

The publisher of this book has preserved the writing style of John Wesley as carefully as possible, including his use of punctuation, capitalization, and King James-era verbs and pronoun forms.

10   9   8   7   6   5   4   3   2   1

To my wife,
Vanessa:
the only one
other than God himself
able to warm my heart

PREFACE

This book is designed for all those for whom spiritual growth and formation is a burning desire. It is intended for the people who wish to discover how John Wesley's interpretation of Scripture and the spiritual life could affect their own.

Wesley believed there were two classes of Christians: those who are weak and often defeated and those who are "first-class." The latter have a relationship with God by faith based on grace alone, but they pay particular attention to the spiritual disciplines (prayer, Scripture reading and meditation, obedience, and the reading of Christ-centered books).

All who are serious about their spiritual growth and formation will benefit by taking this 30-day journey. The text is replete with quotations from John Wesley's letters, journals, prayers, and sermons. An opportunity is given with each day's reading to apply any insights gained to life through prayer and journaling suggestions.

INTRODUCTION

The following devotional readings are taken from the sermons, letters, journals, and prayers of John Wesley, our spiritual forefather and the founder of the Methodist movement.

Wesley was born in 1703 and died in 1791 in England. He was an uncommon revival preacher and social reformer. At the time of his birth and early life, England was a place of poverty, squalor, and sin. By the time of his death the power of God had touched the very life of a nation with revival, changing its very destiny—due in large part to Wesley's spiritual fervor and genius. You will experience some of that fervor and genius on this 30-day journey.

Wesley was a "radical optimist"* when it came to his beliefs concerning what the grace of God could do in the life of individuals. He believed in turning the heathen into converts and converts into saints.

This is an experiment in "spiritual reading." For 30 days you will be spending time in the company of this radical optimist. First, read the article titled "Growing in Holiness—Through Spiritual Reading." It will give you practical counsel on the nature of the discipline of spiritual reading. Then, once a day, make some quiet time to practice leisurely and meditative reflection. Try to follow the article's suggestions as you read the devotionals that follow. Do not hurry! Haste is a prime enemy of holiness. Between the scripture, prayers, and spiritual reading, there should be something for you to chew on each day.

The day's exercise begins with a short invocational prayer from John Wesley—one each week for your reflection. Next comes a scripture meditation from Paul's letter to the Ephesians. Then follows a passage from Wesley's writings. Following your meditation, I would encourage you to take time for personal prayer, both extemporaneous and by using the written prayer of Wesley. Most of us are not used to what is known as "forms of prayer" or praying written prayers. But you will find the discipline of praying these written prayers to be extremely helpful.

Finally, try to do the journaling exercise at least two or three times a week. Your journal can be a spiral-bound notebook or a leather-bound blank book—it does not matter as long as you reflectively write concerning the intersection of your soul's journey and Wesley's writing.

---

*This term is borrowed from Wesley D. Tracy et al., *The Upward Call: Spiritual Formation and the Holy Life* (Kansas City: Beacon Hill Press of Kansas City, 1994), 35 ff.

GROWING IN HOLINESS— THROUGH SPIRITUAL READING

In the state of Arizona, where I live, there is a beautiful national monument near Flagstaff called Walnut Canyon. Among the amazing features of this area are the ancient dwellings built beneath natural overhangs in the limestone and sandstone cliffs. These structures, 33 in all, were built by the Sinaqua Indians over eight centuries ago.

In order to view the dwellings with their smoke-stained walls and tiny doors, one must first climb down over 200 steps from the edge of the canyon. Imagine walking down 240 steps and 800 years into the past. Imagine, still, climbing back up those steps and into the present! It is quite a breathtaking experience.

I do something like this every time I pick up my Bible or another good book; I step into the past and learn from its residents. I have had a growing love affair with books for many years. It has been only recently, however, that I have discovered how best to benefit from them.

Most of my reading had been for information. Sometimes I read for motivation. I am learning now to read also for *transformation*.

Reading for transformation has always been a standard element for spiritual growth. Traditionally it has been called *lectio divina*, a Latin phrase meaning "divine reading" or "sacred reading." Today's student of the spiritual disciplines calls it "spiritual reading," "reading for formation," or "reading for holiness." At its best, spiritual reading is sitting at the feet of those who have walked the way before us and learning from them. Reading for transformation becomes reading for companionship. It is reading that ultimately leads to prayer.

The Bible, of course, is our primary book for spiritual reading. The apostle Paul assures us that "all Scripture is God-breathed and is useful for teaching, rebuking, correcting and training in righteousness, so that the man of God may be thoroughly equipped for every good work" (2 Tim. 3:16-17, NIV).

Spiritual reading also includes solid Christ-centered books. John Wesley continually encouraged his Methodists to read. He was so convinced of the benefits of the discipline that he abridged and reprinted many of the books that had been his own companions along the way into a series called *A Christian Library*. To a divinity student Wesley suggested meeting with a small group to "read the closest and most searching books you can, and apply them honestly to each other's heart" (Telford, ed., *Letters*, 3:207, December 4, 1756).

This kind of reading demands certain skills that reading for information or motivation does not. In our hasty "grab and gobble" society we must acquire or recover the basic skills of leisurely, reflective, and repetitive reading. Someone has likened spiritual reading to sucking on a lozenge rather than gulping a meal.

John Wesley recognized the demand for these special reading skills. Here is a summary of his "Advice on Spiritual Reading":

1. Plan a specific time each day for spiritual reading, and, as far as possible, stick to it.
2. Prepare yourself for reading by *(a)* intentionally reading for the good of your spiritual life and *(b)* praying that God would enable you to see and do His will discovered in what you read.
3. Be sure to read leisurely, seriously, and with attentiveness rather than skimming hastily.
4. Pause often and allow time for God's grace to shed light on your reading.

5. Consider every now and then how you might put into practice that about which God is speaking to you.
6. Whatever book you begin, read through to the end. Read and reread passages that speak to your needs.
7. Put yourself into your reading, allowing it to warm your heart as well as enlighten your mind.
8. Select pertinent quotations for memorization.
9. Conclude your reading with a short prayer to God that He would bless it to your soul's good.

Following are two simple exercises you might try in order to incorporate reading for holiness into your life. Take your time as you begin spiritual reading. You are not reading for information or motivation but rather for transformation.

Spiritual Reading of Scripture

1. Find a quiet place away from telephone, television, and visitors.
2. Select a short passage of Scripture (two or three verses).
3. Read the verses, and then read them again. Finally, read them out loud, savoring every word.
4. Repeat a verse over and over, emphasizing a different word or phrase each time. For example: "Bless the Lord, O my soul" (Ps. 103:1) could be repeated as "BLESS the Lord, O my soul," "Bless THE LORD, O my soul," "Bless the Lord, O MY soul," and finally "Bless the Lord, O my SOUL."

Spiritual Reading of Christian Literature

1. Find a quiet place away from telephone, television, and visitors.
2. Begin reading in a selected Christ-centered book.
3. Read slowly, leisurely, reflectively.

4. When you come to a sentence or paragraph that especially speaks to you, stop. Read it again. Perhaps read it aloud, softly.
5. Apply the truth of the passage to your life. Is there any change you must make, a fault to correct, or grace to claim? Commit yourself to obedience!
6. If you enjoy journaling, copy the sentence or paragraph into your journal, or reflect on it in your journal.
7. Begin to memorize a favorite sentence from the passage.
8. Thank the Lord for your insight, and either continue reading or go about your day.

Through spiritual reading you can enjoy walking down the steps into the past and conversing with those who have walked with Jesus before you. You can enjoy climbing back into the present, knowing, by God's grace and help, you are a better person.

Suggestions for Spiritual Reading

Basics
1. The Holy Bible
2. *Disciplines for the Inner Life*, by Bob Benson and Michael W. Benson

Classics
1. *Confessions*, by Augustine
2. *The Pilgrim's Progress*, by John Bunyan*

Holiness Spirituality
1. *The Christian's Secret of a Happy Life*, by Hannah Whitall Smith*
2. *A Plain Account of Christian Perfection*, by John Wesley*

Modern Spirituality
1. *The Celebration of Discipline*, by Richard J. Foster*

2. *Hinds' Feet on High Places,* by Hannah Hurnard*
3. *The Pursuit of God,* by A. W. Tozer, published by Christian Publications

Fiction and Poetry
1. *Wesley Hymns,* compiled by Ken Bible*
2. *The Screwtape Letters,* by C. S. Lewis*

---

*Available from Beacon Hill Press of Kansas City: 800-877-0700

DAY 1

INVOCATION: *Almighty God, unto whom all hearts be open, all desires known, and from whom no secrets are hid. Cleanse the thoughts of our hearts by the inspiration of thy Holy Spirit, that we may perfectly love thee, and worthily magnify thy holy name, through Christ our Lord, Amen.*

—from the Collect for the Communion Service

The Book of Worship for Church and Home (Nashville: Methodist Publishing House, 1964), 16.

SCRIPTURE MEDITATION: Eph. 1:3-10

A Heart Strangely Warmed

In the evening I went very unwillingly to a society in Aldersgate-Street, where one was reading Luther's preface to the Epistle to the Romans. About a quarter before nine, while he was describing the change which God works in the heart through faith in Christ, I felt my heart strangely warmed. I felt I did trust in Christ, Christ alone for salvation: And an assurance was given me, that he had taken away *my* sins, even *mine*, and saved *me* from the law of sin and death.

—Wesley's journal, May 24, 1738

John Wesley, *The Works of John Wesley*, 3rd ed., 14 vols. (Kansas City: Beacon Hill Press of Kansas City, 1978-79 reprint of 1872 edition), 1:103.

A PRAYER OF JOHN WESLEY:
Forgive them all, O Lord:
our sins of omission and our sins of commission;
the sins of our youth and the sins of our riper years,
the sins of our souls and the sins of our bodies;
our secret sins of ignorance and surprise,
and our more deliberate and presumptuous sins;

> *the sins we have done to please ourselves
> and the sins we have done to please others;
> the sins we know and remember,
> and the sins we have forgotten;
> the sins we have striven to hide from others
> and the sins by which we have made others offend;
> forgive them, O Lord, forgive them all for his sake,
> who died for our sins and rose for our justification
> and now stands at thy right hand
> to make intercession for us,
> Jesus Christ our Lord. AMEN.*

_{Eerdmans' Book of Famous Prayers, comp. Veronica Zundell (Grand Rapids: William B. Eerdmans Publishing Co., reprinted 1985), 62. See also *John Wesley's Prayers*, ed. Frederick C. Gill (New York: Abingdon-Cokesbury Press, 1951), 117-18.}

PERSONAL PRAYER

JOURNAL ENTRY: Take a few moments to reflect and write about a time when your heart was strangely warmed.

DAY 2

INVOCATION: *Almighty God, unto whom all hearts be open, all desires known, and from whom no secrets are hid. Cleanse the thoughts of our hearts by the inspiration of thy Holy Spirit, that we may perfectly love thee, and worthily magnify thy holy name, through Christ our Lord, Amen.*

—from the Collect for the Communion Service
The Book of Worship for Church and Home, 16.

SCRIPTURE MEDITATION: Eph. 1:11-14

Remarkable Providence

The following letter, written by my mother, gives an account of a very remarkable providence: But it is imperfect with regard to me. That part none but I myself can supply. Her account, wrote to a neighbouring Clergyman, begins:—

"EPWORTH, *August* 24, 1709.

"On Wednesday night, February 9, between the hours of eleven and twelve, some sparks fell from the roof of our house, upon one of the children's (Hetty's) feet. She immediately ran to our chamber, and called us. Mr. Wesley, hearing a cry of fire in the street, started up, . . . and, opening his door, found the fire was in his own house. He immediately . . . bid me and my two eldest daughters rise quickly and shift for ourselves. Then he ran and burst open the nursery-door, and called to the maid to bring out the children. The two little ones lay in the bed with her; the three others in another bed. She snatched up the youngest, and bid the rest follow; which the three elder did. When we were got into the hall, and were surrounded with flames, Mr. Wesley found he had left the keys of the doors above stairs. He ran up, and recovered them, a minute before the staircase took fire. When we opened the street-door, the strong north-east wind drove the flames in with such violence, that none could stand against them. But some of our children got out through the windows, the rest through a little door into the garden. I was not in a condition to climb up to the windows; neither could I get to the garden-door. I endeavoured three times to force my passage through the street-door, but was as often beat back by the fury of the flames. In this distress, I besought our blessed Saviour for help, and then waded through the fire, naked as I was, which did me no farther harm than a little scorching my hands and my face.

"When Mr. Wesley had seen the other children safe, he heard the child in the nursery cry. He attempted to go up the stairs, but they were all on fire, and would not bear his weight. Finding it impossible to give any help, he kneeled down in the hall, and recommended the soul of the child to God."

I believe, it was just at that time I [John] waked; for I did not cry, as they imagined, unless it was afterwards. I remember all the circumstances as distinctly as though it were but yesterday. Seeing the room was very light, I called to the maid to take me up. But none answering, I put my head out of the curtains, and saw streaks of fire on the top of the room. I got up and ran to the door, but could get no farther, all the floor beyond it being in a blaze. I then climbed up on a chest which stood near the window: One in the yard saw me, and proposed running to fetch a ladder. Another answered, "There will not be time . . . Here, I will fix myself against the wall; lift a light man, and set him on my shoulders." They did so, and he took me out of the window. Just then the whole roof fell in; but it fell inward, or we had been all crushed at once. When they brought me into the house where my father was, he cried out, "Come, neighbours, let us kneel down! Let us give thanks to God! He has given me all my eight children: Let the house go; I am rich enough."

The next day, as he was walking in the garden, and surveying the ruins of the house, he picked up part of a leaf of his polyglott Bible, on which just those words were legible: *Vade; vende omnia quoe habes, et attolle crucem, et sequere me.* "Go, sell all that thou hast; and take up thy cross, and follow me."

The Works of John Wesley, 13:516-18.

A Prayer of John Wesley:
From all manner of evil, but especially from sin; from all occasions of offending the divine majesty and from the particular temptation to which by time, place or temper we are most exposed; Deliver us, O Lord. Amen.

John Wesley's Prayers, 118.

PERSONAL PRAYER

JOURNAL ENTRY: React to what Wesley's father said: "Let the house go; I am rich enough."

DAY 3

INVOCATION: *Almighty God, unto whom all hearts be open, all desires known, and from whom no secrets are hid. Cleanse the thoughts of our hearts by the inspiration of thy Holy Spirit, that we may perfectly love thee, and worthily magnify thy holy name, through Christ our Lord, Amen.*

—from the Collect for the Communion Service
The Book of Worship for Church and Home, 16.

SCRIPTURE MEDITATION: Eph. 1:15-23

Jesus Christ

About noon I preached at Warrington; I am afraid, not to the taste of some of my hearers, as my subject led me to speak strongly and explicitly on the Godhead of Christ. But that I cannot help; for on this I *must* insist, as the foundation of all our hope.

—Wesley's journal, Tuesday, April 5, 1768
The Works of John Wesley, 3:315.

I believe that Jesus of Nazareth was the Saviour of the world, the Messiah so long foretold; that, being anointed with the Holy Ghost, he was a Prophet, revealing to us the whole will of God; that he was a Priest, who gave himself a sacrifice for sin, and still makes intercession for transgressors; that he is a King, who has all power in heaven and in earth, and will reign till he has subdued all things to himself.

I believe he is the proper, natural Son of God, God of God, very God of very God; and that he is the Lord of all, having absolute, supreme, universal dominion over all things; but more peculiarly our Lord, who believe in him, both by conquest, purchase, and voluntary obligation.

I believe that he was made man, joining the human nature with the divine in one person; being conceived by the singular operation of the Holy Ghost, and born of the blessed Virgin Mary.

I believe he suffered inexpressible pains of both body and soul, and at last death, even the death of the cross, at the time that Pontius Pilate governed Judea, under the Roman Emperor; that his body was then laid in the grave, and his soul went to the place of separate spirits; that the third day he rose again from the dead; that he ascended into heaven; where he remains in the midst of the throne of God, in the highest power and glory, as Mediator till the end of the world, as God to all eternity; that, in the end, he will come down from heaven, to judge every man according to his works; both those who shall be then alive, and all who have died before that day.

—from "A Letter to a Roman Catholic"
The Works of John Wesley, 10:81-82.

A PRAYER OF JOHN WESLEY:
O Jesus, poor and abject, unknown and despised, have mercy upon me, and let me not be ashamed to follow thee.

O Jesus, hated, calumniated, and persecuted, have mercy upon me, and let me not be ashamed to come after thee.

O Jesus, betrayed and sold at a vile price, have mercy upon me, and make me content to be as my Master.

O Jesus, blasphemed, accused, and wrongfully condemned, have mercy upon me, and teach me to endure the contradiction of sinners.

O Jesus, clothed with a habit of reproach and shame, have mercy upon me, and let me not seek my own glory.

O Jesus, insulted, mocked, and spit upon, have mercy upon me, and let me run with patience the race set before me.

O Jesus, dragged to the pillar, scourged, and bathed in blood, have mercy upon me, and let me not faint in the fiery trial.

O Jesus, crowned with thorns, and hailed in derision;

O Jesus, burdened with our sins, and the curses of the people;

O Jesus, affronted, outraged, buffeted, overwhelmed with injuries, griefs, and humiliations;

O Jesus, hanging on the accursed tree, bowing the head, giving up the ghost, have mercy upon me, and conform my whole soul to thy holy, humble, suffering Spirit. AMEN.

—from "A Collection of Forms of Prayer, for Every Day in the Week"

The Works of John Wesley, 11:229.

PERSONAL PRAYER

JOURNAL ENTRY: How does the above prayer affect you?

DAY 4

INVOCATION: *Almighty God, unto whom all hearts be open, all desires known, and from whom no secrets are hid. Cleanse the thoughts of our hearts by the inspiration of thy Holy Spirit, that we may perfectly love thee, and worthily magnify thy holy name, through Christ our Lord, Amen.*

—from the Collect for the Communion Service

The Book of Worship for Church and Home, 16.

SCRIPTURE MEDITATION: Eph. 1:15-23

Prayer

It is certain the Scripture by "prayer" almost always means vocal prayer. And whosoever intermits [neglects] this for any time, will neither pray with the voice nor the heart. It is therefore our wisdom to force ourselves to prayer; to pray whether we can pray or not. And many times while we are so doing, the fire will fall from heaven, and we shall know our labour was not in vain.

—letter to Miss Bishop, September 19, 1773
The Works of John Wesley, 13:25.

Have I prayed with fervour? At going in and out of church? In church? Morning and evening in private? With my friends? Without ceasing? Have I sincerely meant every word of my prayers? Have I prayed with humility, admitting my inability to pray? Have I concluded my prayers in the Savior's Name, recognizing that he intercedes for me at the right hand of God?

Have I during the day prayed for humility, faith, hope, love? Do I love my fellowman, do I deny self and am I truly thankful? Have I offered all I do to my Redeemer, begged his assistance in even the small acts, commended my soul to his keeping? Have I done all this carefully (not in haste), seriously (not allowing any interruptions), and as fervently as I could?

Devotions and Prayers of John Wesley, ed. Donald E. Demaray (Grand Rapids: Baker Book House, 1957), 22.

"Pray without ceasing."

—from the flyleaf of Wesley's private diary

A PRAYER OF JOHN WESLEY:
Take thou the full possession of my heart; raise there thy throne, and command there as thou dost in heaven. Being created by thee, let me live to thee; being created for thee, let me ever act for thy glory; being redeemed by thee, let me render unto thee what

is thine, and let my spirit ever cleave to thee alone. AMEN.
—from "A Collection of Forms of Prayer,
for Every Day in the Week"
The Works of John Wesley, 11:205.

PERSONAL PRAYER

JOURNAL ENTRY: Answer some of Mr. Wesley's self-examination questions.

DAY 5

INVOCATION: *Almighty God, unto whom all hearts be open, all desires known, and from whom no secrets are hid. Cleanse the thoughts of our hearts by the inspiration of thy Holy Spirit, that we may perfectly love thee, and worthily magnify thy holy name, through Christ our Lord, Amen.*
—from the Collect for the Communion Service
The Book of Worship for Church and Home, 16.

SCRIPTURE MEDITATION: Eph. 1:11-14; 2:8-10

Created in Christ Jesus to Do Good Works

Dear Sir,

I am glad that it has pleased God to restore your health, and that you have been employing it to the best of purposes. It is worth living for this, (and scarcely for anything else), to testify the Gospel of the grace of God. You will find many in these parts who have ears and hearts to receive even the deep things of God.

—from a letter to Robert Carr Brackenbury, Esq., June 23, 1780
The Works of John Wesley, 13:1-2.

And who would wish to live for any meaner purpose than to serve God in our generation? I know my health and strength are continued for this very thing. And if ever I should listen to that siren song, "Spare thyself," I believe my Master would spare me no longer, but soon take me away. It pleases Him to deal with you in a different way. He frequently calls you not so much to act as to suffer. And you may well say,—

> "O take thy way! Thy way is best:
> Grant or deny me ease.
> This is but tuning of my breast
> To make the music please."

I am glad you are still determined to do what you can, and to do it without delay.

—from a letter to the same, January 10, 1783
The Works of John Wesley, 13:4.

"But what good works are those, the practice of which you affirm to be necessary to sanctification?" First, all works of piety; such as public prayer, family prayer, and praying in our closet; receiving the supper of the Lord; searching the Scriptures, by hearing, reading, meditating; and using such a measure of fasting or abstinence as our bodily health allows.

Secondly, all works of mercy; whether they relate to the bodies or souls of men; such as feeding the hungry, clothing the naked, entertaining the stranger, visiting those that are in prison, or sick, or variously afflicted; such as the endeavouring to instruct the ignorant, to awaken the stupid sinner, to quicken the lukewarm, to confirm the wavering, to comfort the feeble-minded, to succour the tempted, or contribute in any manner to the saving of souls from death. This is the repentance, and these the "fruits meet for repentance," which are necessary to full sanctification. This is the way wherein God hath appointed his children to wait for complete salvation....

... But he cannot be sanctified without faith. Likewise,

let a man have ever so much of this repentance, or ever so many good works, yet all this does not . . . avail: He is not sanctified till he believes. But the moment he believes, with or without those fruits, yea, with more or less of this repentance, he is sanctified.—Not in the *same sense;* for this repentance and these fruits are only *remotely* necessary,—necessary in order to the continuance of his faith, as well as the increase of it; whereas faith is *immediately* and *directly* necessary to sanctification.
—from Wesley's sermon "The Scripture Way of Salvation"
The Works of John Wesley, 6:51-52.

A PRAYER OF JOHN WESLEY:
O thou Giver of every good and perfect gift, if at any time thou pleasest to work by my hand, teach me to discern what is my own from what is another's, and to render unto thee the things that are thine. As all the good that is done on earth thou doest it thyself, let me ever return to thee all the glory. Let me, as a pure crystal, transmit all the light thou pourest upon me. AMEN.
—from "A Collection of Forms of Prayer, for Every Day in the Week"
The Works of John Wesley, 11:217.

PERSONAL PRAYER

JOURNAL ENTRY: Take a moment to write what it means to you to live "for the praise of his glory" (Eph. 1:12, NIV).

DAY 6

INVOCATION: *Almighty God, unto whom all hearts be open, all desires known, and from whom no secrets are hid. Cleanse the thoughts of our hearts by the inspiration of thy Holy Spirit, that we may perfectly love thee, and worthily magnify thy holy name, through Christ our Lord, Amen.*

—from the Collect for the Communion Service
The Book of Worship for Church and Home, 16.

SCRIPTURE MEDITATION: Eph. 2:1-10

Come to Christ!

My dear Lady,

. . . I cannot but think of you often: I seem to see you . . . panting after God . . . convinced that you are a sinner, a debtor that has nothing to pay, and just ready to cry out,

"Jesu, now I have lost my all,
Let me upon thy bosom fall."

Amen, Lord Jesus! Speak, for thy servant heareth! Speak thyself into her heart! Lift up the hands that hang down, and the feeble knees. Let her see thee full of grace and truth, and make her glad with the light of thy countenance.

Do not stop, my dear Lady, one moment, "because you have not felt sorrow enough." Your Friend above has felt enough of it for you.

O Lamb of God, was ever pain,
Was ever love like thine!

Look, look unto him, and be thou saved! He is not a God afar off; he is now hovering over you with eyes of tenderness and love! Only believe! Then he turns your heaviness into joy. Do not think you are not humble enough, not contrite enough, not earnest enough. You are nothing; but Christ is all, and he is yours. The Lord God write it upon your heart, and take you for an habitation of God through the Spirit.

. . . But, O! take Christ to-day! I long to have you happy in him! Surely, few have a more earnest desire of your happiness than,

> My very dear Lady,
>> Your Ladyship's most affectionate servant,
>>> John Wesley
>>>> —from a letter to Lady Maxwell, July 10, 1764
>>>>> *The Works of John Wesley,* 12:335-36.

A PRAYER OF JOHN WESLEY:
My Lord and my God, thou seest my heart, and my desires are not hid from thee. . . .

I am ashamed when I think how long I have lived a stranger . . . to thee. . . .

Lord, hear me, help me, and show mercy unto me, for Jesus Christ's sake.

To thee, O God, Father, Son, and Holy Ghost, my Creator, Redeemer, and Sanctifier, I give up myself entirely; May I no longer serve myself, but thee, all the days of my life. . . . Amen.
—from "A Collection of Forms of Prayer, for Every Day in the Week"
The Works of John Wesley, 11:226, 228.

PERSONAL PRAYER

JOURNAL ENTRY: Reflect a few moments on the heartbeat of a man who would write a letter such as this.

DAY 7

INVOCATION: *Almighty God, unto whom all hearts be open, all desires known, and from whom no secrets are hid. Cleanse the thoughts of our hearts by the inspiration of thy Holy Spirit, that we may perfectly love thee, and worthily magnify thy holy name, through Christ our Lord, Amen.*

—from the Collect for the Communion Service
The Book of Worship for Church and Home, 16.

SCRIPTURE MEDITATION: Eph. 2:11-22

A New Creature

"If any man be in Christ, he is a new creature: Old things are passed away; behold, all things are become new."

First: His Judgments are new: His judgment of *himself*, of *happiness*, of *holiness*.

He judges himself to be altogether fallen short of the glorious image of God: To have no good thing abiding in him; but all that is corrupt and abominable; In a word, to be wholly earthly, sensual, and devilish;—a motley mixture of beast and devil.

Thus, by the grace of God in Christ, I judge of myself. Therefore I am, in this respect, a new creature.

Again: His judgment concerning *happiness* is new. He would as soon expect to dig it out of the earth, as to find it in riches, honour, pleasure, (so called,) or indeed in the enjoyment of any creature: He knows there can be no happiness on earth, but in the enjoyment of God, and in the foretaste of those "rivers of pleasure which flow at his right hand for evermore."

Thus, by the grace of God in Christ, I judge of happiness. Therefore I am, in this respect, a new creature.

Yet again: His judgment concerning *holiness* is new. He no longer judges it to be an outward thing: To consist either in doing no harm, in doing good, or in using the ordinances of God. He sees it is the life of God in the soul; the image of God fresh stamped on the heart; an entire renewal of the mind in every temper and thought, after the likeness of Him that created it.

Thus by the grace of God in Christ, I judge of holiness. Therefore I am, in this respect, a new creature.

—Wesley's journal, Saturday, October 14, 1738
The Works of John Wesley, 1:161.

A PRAYER OF JOHN WESLEY:
O thou all-sufficient God of angels and men, who art above all, and through all, and in all; from whom, by whom, and in whom are all things; "in whom we live, move, and have our being;" may my will be as entirely and continually derived from thine, as my being and happiness are! AMEN.

—from "A Collection of Forms of Prayer, for Every Day in the Week"
The Works of John Wesley, 11:224.

PERSONAL PRAYER

JOURNAL ENTRY: Take a few moments to give your description of a "new creature" in Christ. Pause to compare yours with Wesley's, and then go about your day.

DAY 8

INVOCATION: *O blessed Lord, enable me to fulfil thy commands, and command what thou wilt.* AMEN.

—from "A Collection of Forms of Prayer, for Every Day in the Week"
The Works of John Wesley, 11:214.

SCRIPTURE MEDITATION: Eph. 3:1-13

A Man of One Book

To candid, reasonable men, I am not afraid to lay open what have been the inmost thoughts of my heart. I have thought, I am a creature of a day, passing through life as an arrow through the air. I am a spirit come from God, and returning to God: Just hovering over the great gulf; till, a few moments hence, I am no more seen; I drop into an unchangeable eternity! I want to know one thing,—the way to heaven; how to land safe on that happy shore. God himself has condescended to teach the way: For this very end he came from heaven. He hath written it down in a book. O give me that book! At any price, give me the book of God! I have it: Here is knowledge enough for me. Let me be *homo unius libri* (a man of one book). Here then I am, far from the busy ways of men. I sit down alone: Only God is here. In his presence I open, I read his book; for this end, to find the way to heaven. Is there a doubt concerning the meaning of what I read? Does anything appear dark or intricate? I lift up my heart to the Father of Lights:—"Lord, is it not thy word, 'If any man lack wisdom, let him ask of God?' Thou 'givest liberally, and upbraidest not.' Thou hast said, 'If any be willing to do thy will, he shall know.' I am willing to do, let me know, thy will." I then search after and consider parallel passages of Scripture, "comparing spiritual things with spiritual." I meditate thereon with all the attention and earnestness of which my mind is capable. If any doubt still remains, I consult those who are experienced in the things of God; and then the writings whereby, being dead, they yet speak. And what I thus learn, that I teach.

—from "Preface to the Sermons"
The Works of John Wesley, 5:2-4.

A Prayer of John Wesley:
We offer up again our souls and bodies to thee to be governed, not by our will, but thine. O let it be ever the ease and joy of our

hearts, to be under the conduct of thy unerring wisdom, to follow thy counsels, and to be ruled in all things by thy holy will. And let us never distrust thy abundant kindness and tender care over us; whatsoever it is thou wouldest have us to do or to suffer in this world. AMEN.

—from "A Collection of Prayers for Families"
The Works of John Wesley, 11:239.

PERSONAL PRAYER

JOURNAL ENTRY: Take a few moments to put the closing prayer above into your own words.

DAY 9

INVOCATION: *O blessed Lord, enable me to fulfil thy commands, and command what thou wilt. AMEN.*

—from "A Collection of Forms of Prayer, for Every Day in the Week"
The Works of John Wesley, 11:214.

SCRIPTURE MEDITATION: Eph. 3:14-21

Rooted and Grounded in Love

My dear Betsy,

. . . we know, there is nothing deeper, there is nothing better, in heaven or earth, than love! There cannot be, unless there were something higher than the God of love! So that we see distinctly what we have to aim at. We see the prize, and the way to it! Here is the height, here is the depth, of Christian experience! "God is love; and he that dwelleth in love, dwelleth in God, and God in him."

>   —from a letter to Miss Ritchie, January 17, 1775
>   *The Works of John Wesley*, 13:55.

By Christian perfection, I mean (as I have said again and again) the so loving God and our neighbour, as to "rejoice evermore, pray without ceasing, and in everything give thanks." He that experiences this, is scripturally perfect. And if you do not, yet you may experience it: You surely will, if you follow hard after it; for the Scripture cannot be broken.

>   —from a letter to Mrs. Maitland, May 12, 1763
>   *The Works of John Wesley*, 12:257.

My dear Miss Loxdale,

I advised formerly my dear Jenny Cooper, and so I advise you, frequently to read and meditate upon the thirteenth chapter of the First Epistle to the Corinthians. There is the true picture of Christian perfection! Let us copy after it with all our might. I believe it might likewise be of use to you to read more than once the "Plain Account of Christian Perfection." Indeed, what is it more or less than humble, gentle, patient love! It is undoubtedly our privilege to "rejoice evermore," with a calm, still, heartfelt joy. Nevertheless, this is seldom long at one stay. Many circumstances may cause it to ebb and flow. This, therefore, is not the essence of religion; which is no other than humble, gentle, patient love. I do not know whether all these are not included in that one word, resignation. For the highest lesson our Lord (as man) learned on earth was to say, "Not as I will, but as thou wilt."—May He confirm you more and more!

>   Yours most affectionately,
>   John Wesley
>   —letter to Miss Loxdale, April 12, 1782
>   *The Works of John Wesley*, 13:130-31.

A PRAYER OF JOHN WESLEY:
O my God, fill my soul with so entire a love of thee, that I may love nothing but for thy sake, and in subordination to thy love. AMEN.

The Works of John Wesley, 11:212.

PERSONAL PRAYER

JOURNAL ENTRY: What does it mean to you to be rooted and grounded in love?

DAY 10

INVOCATION: *O blessed Lord, enable me to fulfil thy commands, and command what thou wilt. AMEN.*

—from "A Collection of Forms of Prayer, for Every Day in the Week"
The Works of John Wesley, 11:214.

SCRIPTURE MEDITATION: Eph. 3:20-21

He Is Able

Absolute or infallible perfection I never contended for. Sinless perfection I do not contend for, seeing it is not scriptural. A perfection, such as enables a person to fulfil the whole law, and so needs not the merits of Christ,—I acknowledge no such perfection; I do now, and always did, protest against it.

"But is there no sin in those who are perfect in love?" I believe not: But be that as it may, they feel none; no temper contrary to pure love, while they rejoice, pray, and give thanks continually. And whether sin is suspended, or extinguished, I will not dispute: It is enough that they feel nothing but love. This you allow we should daily press after. And this is all I contend for. O may the Lord give you to taste of it to-day!

—from a letter to Mrs. Maitland, May 12, 1763
The Works of John Wesley, 12:257-58.

Dear Sister,

... The plain fact is this: I know many who love God with all their heart, mind, soul, and strength. He is their one desire, their one delight, and they are continually happy in him. They love their neighbour as themselves. They feel as sincere, fervent, constant a desire for the happiness of every man, good or bad, friend or enemy, as for their own. They "rejoice evermore, pray without ceasing, and in everything give thanks." Their souls are continually streaming up to God in holy joy, prayer, and praise. This is plain, sound, scriptural experience: And of this we have more and more living witnesses.

But these souls dwell in a shattered, corruptible body, and are so pressed down thereby, that they cannot exert their love as they would, by always thinking, speaking, and acting precisely right. For want of better bodily organs, they sometimes inevitably think, speak, or act wrong. Yet I think they need the advocacy of Christ, even for these involuntary defects; although they do not imply a defect of love, but of understanding.... So that, even to such, strong cautions are needful. After the heart is cleansed from pride, anger, and desire, it may suffer them to re-enter: Therefore I have long thought some expressions in the Hymns are abundantly too strong; as I cannot perceive any state mentioned in Scripture from which we may not (in a measure, at least) fall....

Forgive me, dear Miss Hardy, that I do but just touch upon the heads of your letter. Indeed, this defect does not spring from the want of love, but only from want of time. I should not wonder if your soul was one of the next that

was filled with pure love. Receive it freely, thou poor bruised reed! It is able to make thee stand.
>—from a letter to Miss Elizabeth Hardy, December 26, 1761
>*The Works of John Wesley*, 12:235-36.

A PRAYER OF JOHN WESLEY:
Pardon, good Lord, all my former sins, and make me every day more zealous and diligent to improve every opportunity of building up my soul in thy faith, and love, and obedience. Make thyself always present to my mind, and let thy love fill and rule my soul, in all those places, and companies, and employments to which thou callest me this day. AMEN.
>—from "A Collection of Forms of Prayer, for Every Day in the Week"
>*The Works of John Wesley*, 11:210.

PERSONAL PRAYER

JOURNAL ENTRY: Write a letter to Mr. Wesley with your questions.

DAY 11

INVOCATION: *O blessed Lord, enable me to fulfil thy commands, and command what thou wilt.* AMEN.
>—from "A Collection of Forms of Prayer, for Every Day in the Week"
>*The Works of John Wesley*, 11:214.

SCRIPTURE MEDITATION: Eph. 4:1-6

Christian Companions

It gives me pleasure, my dear Fanny, to hear that you still continue in the good way. Still press to the mark, to the prize of the high calling of God in Christ Jesus. From what you have already experienced, you know there is one happiness in the earth below, and in heaven above. You know God alone can satisfy your soul either in earth or heaven. Cleave to Him with full purpose of heart. If you seek happiness in anything but Him, you must be disappointed. I hope you find satisfaction, likewise, in some of your Christian companions. It is a blessed thing to have fellow-travellers to the New Jerusalem. If you cannot find any, you must make them; for none can travel that road alone. Then labour to help each other on, that you may be altogether Christians.

—from a letter to Miss Frances Godfrey, August 2, 1789
The Works of John Wesley, 13:42-43.

I am fully persuaded, if you had always one or two faithful friends near you, who would speak the very truth from their heart, and watch over you in love, you would swiftly advance in running the race which is set before you.

—from a letter to Mr. Ebenezer Blackwell, Wesley's banker, Dublin, July 20, 1752
The Works of John Wesley, 12:178.

The "forbearing one another in love" seems to mean, not only the not resenting anything, and the not avenging yourselves; not only the not injuring, hurting, or grieving each other, either by word or deed; but also the bearing one another's burdens; yea, and lessening them by every means in our power. It implies the sympathizing with them in their sorrows, afflictions, and infirmities; the bearing them up when, without our help, they would be liable to sink under their burdens; the endeavouring to lift their sinking heads, and to strengthen their feeble knees.

—from Wesley's sermon "Of the Church," paragraph 26
The Works of John Wesley, 6:399.

A PRAYER OF JOHN WESLEY:
Be gracious to all who are near and dear to me. Thou knowest their names, and art acquainted with their wants. Of thy goodness be pleased to proportion thy blessings to their necessities. Pardon my enemies, and give them repentance and charity, and me grace to overcome evil with good. Have compassion on all who are distressed in mind, body, or estate, and give them steady patience, and timely deliverance. AMEN.

—from "A Collection of Forms of Prayer, for Every Day in the Week"
The Works of John Wesley, 11:236.

PERSONAL PRAYER

JOURNAL ENTRY: Do you have spiritual traveling companions? A "soul friend"? Share a few moments writing concerning your desire for such a friend as Wesley thinks we need.

DAY 12

INVOCATION: *O blessed Lord, enable me to fulfil thy commands, and command what thou wilt.* AMEN.

—from "A Collection of Forms of Prayer, for Every Day in the Week"
The Works of John Wesley, 11:214.

SCRIPTURE MEDITATION: Eph. 4:1-13

The Church

How much do we almost continually hear about the Church! With many it is a matter of daily conversation.

And yet how few understand what they talk of! how few know what the term means! . . .

. . . "Where two or three are met together in his name," there is Christ; so, (to speak with St. Cyprian,) "where two or three believers are met together, there is a Church." Thus it is that St. Paul, writing to Philemon, mentions "the Church which was in his house;" plainly signifying, that even a Christian family may be termed a Church. . . .

. . . The word Church or Churches means, not the buildings where the Christians assembled, . . . but the people that used to assemble there, one or more Christian congregations. But sometimes the word Church is taken in Scripture in a still more extensive meaning, as including all the Christian congregations that are upon the face of the earth. . . .

Let us consider, First, who are properly the Church of God? What is the true meaning of that term? "The Church . . . ," as the Apostle himself explains it, means, "the saints," the holy persons, that . . . assemble themselves together to worship God the Father, and his Son Jesus Christ . . . it is the Church in general, the catholic or universal Church, which the Apostle . . . considers as one body . . . not only the Christians of one congregation, of one city, of one province, or nation; but all the persons upon the face of the earth, who answer the character here given. . . .

"There is one Spirit" who animates all these, all the living members of the Church of God. . . .

"There is," in all those that have received this Spirit, "one hope;" a hope full of immortality. They know, to die is not to be lost: Their prospect extends beyond the grave. . . .

"There is one Lord," who has now dominion over them; who has set up his kingdom in their hearts, and reigns over all those that are partakers of this hope. To obey him, to run the way of his commandments, is their glory and joy. . . .

"There is one faith;" which is the free gift of God, and is the ground of their hope. This . . . is the faith of St.

Thomas, teaching him to say with holy boldness, "My Lord, and my God!" ...

"There is one baptism;" which is the outward sign ... of all that inward and spiritual grace which he is continually bestowing upon his Church. It is likewise a precious means, whereby this faith and hope are given to those that diligently seek him. ...

"There is one God and Father of all" that have the Spirit of adoption, which "crieth in their hearts, Abba, Father;" which "witnesseth" continually "with their spirits," that they are the children of God: "Who is above all,"—the Most High, the Creator, the Sustainer, the Governor of the whole universe: "And through all,"—pervading all space; filling heaven and earth: ... "And in you all,"—in a peculiar manner living in you. ...

Here, then, is a clear unexceptionable answer to that question, "What is the Church?" The catholic or universal Church is, all the persons in the universe whom God hath so called out of the world as to entitle them to the preceding character; as to be "one body," united by "one Spirit;" having "one faith, one hope, one baptism; one God and Father of all, who is above all, and through all, and in them all."

—from Wesley's sermon "Of the Church"

The Works of John Wesley, 6:392-96.

A PRAYER OF JOHN WESLEY:

We desire, thou knowest, the good of all mankind, especially of all Christian people; that they may all walk worthy of the gospel, and live together in unity and Christian love. AMEN.

—from "A Collection of Prayers for Families"

The Works of John Wesley, 11:242.

PERSONAL PRAYER

JOURNAL ENTRY: How do you react to Mr. Wesley's definition of the Church?

DAY 13

INVOCATION: *O blessed Lord, enable me to fulfil thy commands, and command what thou wilt.* AMEN.

—from "A Collection of Forms of Prayer,
for Every Day in the Week"
The Works of John Wesley, 11:214.

SCRIPTURE MEDITATION: Eph. 4:14-16

Christians of the First Rank

With regard to you, I have frequently observed that there are two very different ranks of Christians, both of whom may be in the favour of God,—a higher and a lower rank. The latter avoid all known sin, do much good, use all the means of grace, but have little of the life of God in their souls, and are much conformed to the world. The former make the Bible their whole rule, and their sole aim is the will and image of God. This they steadily and uniformly pursue, through honour and dishonour, denying themselves, and taking up their cross daily; considering one point only, "How may I attain most of the mind that was in Christ, and how may I please him most?" Now I verily believe, never was a person of rank more prepared for this state than you were the first time I had the pleasure of seeing you. Nay, I doubt not but you pant after it now; your soul is athirst to be all devoted to God. But who will press you forward to this? Rather, who will not draw you back? It is in this respect that I think one that uses plain dealing is needful for you in the highest degree; so needful, that without this help you will inevitably stop short: I do not mean, stop short of heaven; but of that degree of holiness, and, consequently, of happiness both in time and eternity, which is now offered to your acceptance.

It is herein that I am jealous over you. I am afraid of your sinking beneath your calling, degenerating into a common Christian, who shall indeed be saved, but saved as by fire. I long to see both you and your lady a little more than common Christians; Christians of the first rank in the kingdom of God, full of all goodness and truth. I want you to be living witnesses of all Gospel holiness! And what shall hinder, if you seek it by faith? Are not all things ready? The Lord God give you to experience that all things are possible to them that believe!

—from a letter to an anonymous friend, 1770
The Works of John Wesley, 12:250-51.

A Prayer of John Wesley:
O God, let all their life declare,
How happy these thy servants are;
How far above these earthly things;
How pure when wash'd in Jesu's blood;
How intimately one with God,
A heaven-born race of Priests and Kings!
Amen.

—A poem-prayer at the end of the letter above

Personal Prayer

Journal Entry: In which rank of Christians are you?

DAY 14

INVOCATION: *O blessed Lord, enable me to fulfil thy commands, and command what thou wilt. AMEN.*
> —from "A Collection of Forms of Prayer, for Every Day in the Week"
> The Works of John Wesley, 11:214.

SCRIPTURE MEDITATION: Eph. 4:17-24

Tough Words to a Preacher!

I observed long ago, that you are not patient of reproof; and I fear you are less so now than ever. But since you desire it, I will tell you once more what I think, fear, or hear concerning you.

I think you tasted of the powers of the world to come thirteen or fourteen years ago, and [were] then simple of heart, and willing to spend and be spent for Christ. But not long after, not being sufficiently on your guard, you suffered loss by being applauded. This revived and increased your natural vanity; which was the harder to be checked, because of your constitutional stubbornness;—two deadly enemies which have lain in wait for you many years, and have given you many deep, if not mortal, wounds.

I fear . . . you [were] so weakened by these, that you no longer set a watch over your mouth, but began frequently to speak what was not strictly true, to excuse yourself, divert others, or gain applause. I am afraid this has prevailed over you more and more, as there was less and less of the life of God in the soul; so that I should almost wonder if you do not judge a diverting lie to be a very innocent thing.

. . . Being not used to nor fond of reading, and not spending many hours in private prayer, time grew heavy on your hands; . . . So you betook yourself to farming . . .

and grew more and more dead to God. Especially when you began to keep company . . . with the men . . . who have little to do either with religion or reason; and have but just wit enough to smoke, drink, and flatter you.

By these dull wretches you have been an unspeakable loser. . . .

O remember from whence you are fallen? Repent, and do the first works! First recover the life of God in your own soul, and walk as Christ walked. Walk with God as you did twelve years ago. Then you might again be useful to his children. . . . I have now told you all that is in my heart: I hope you will receive it, not only with patience, but profit.

You must be much in the way, or much out of the way; a good soldier for God, or for the devil. O choose the better part!—now!—today!

—from a letter to Mr. John Trembath, September 21, 1755
The Works of John Wesley, 12:251-53.

A PRAYER OF JOHN WESLEY:
Strengthen all thy faithful servants. Bring back them that wander out of the way; raise up those that are fallen; confirm those that stand, and grant them steadily to persevere in faith, love, and obedience. AMEN.

—from "A Collection of Prayers for Families"
The Works of John Wesley, 11:250.

PERSONAL PRAYER

JOURNAL ENTRY: How would you react to receiving a letter like this?

DAY 15

INVOCATION: *Almighty and everlasting God, . . . mercifully this day watch over me with the eyes of thy mercy. Direct my soul and body according to the rule of thy will, and fill my heart with thy Holy Spirit, that I may pass this day, and all the rest of my days, to thy glory.* AMEN.
—from "A Collection of Forms of Prayer,
for Every Day in the Week"
The Works of John Wesley, 11:228.

SCRIPTURE MEDITATION: Eph. 4:25-28

On Entering the Church
ENTER THIS DOOR
AS IF THE FLOOR
  WITHIN WERE GOLD
AND EVERY WALL
OF JEWELS, ALL
  OF WEALTH UNTOLD;
AS IF THE CHOIR
IN ROBE OF FIRE
  WERE SINGING HERE
NOR SHOUT, NOR RUSH
BUT HUSH—
  FOR GOD IS HERE.
—engraved on the floor of the church
where John Wesley preached his first sermon

A PRAYER OF JOHN WESLEY:
PRAYER OF SELF-DONATION
O Lord Jesu,
I give thee my body,
my soul,
my substance,

> *my fame,*
> *my friends,*
> *my liberty,*
> *my life:*
> *Dispose of me,*
> *and all that is mine,*
> *as it seemeth best unto thee.*
> *I am not mine, but thine;*
> *Claim me as thy right,*
> *keep me as thy charge,*
> *love me as thy child!*
> *Fight for me when I am assaulted,*
> *[and] heal me when I am wounded.*
> AMEN.
>
> —from "A Collection of Forms of Prayer,
> for Every Day in the Week"
> The Works of John Wesley, 11:224.

PERSONAL PRAYER

JOURNAL ENTRY: Reflect on how you enter the church sanctuary.

DAY 16

INVOCATION: *Almighty and everlasting God, . . . mercifully this day watch over me with the eyes of thy mercy. Direct my soul and body according to the rule of thy will, and fill my heart with thy Holy Spirit, that I may pass this day, and all the rest of my days, to thy glory.* AMEN.

—from "A Collection of Forms of Prayer,
for Every Day in the Week"
The Works of John Wesley, 11:228.

Scripture Meditation: Eph. 4:25-32

Be Kind and Compassionate to One Another
DO ALL THE GOOD YOU CAN
BY ALL THE MEANS YOU CAN
IN ALL THE WAYS YOU CAN
IN ALL THE PLACES YOU CAN
IN ALL THE TIMES YOU CAN
TO ALL THE PEOPLE YOU CAN
AS LONG AS EVER YOU CAN.

John Wesley on "works" from *Living Quotations for Christians*, ed. Sherwood Eliot Wirt and Kersten Beckstrom (New York: Harper and Row, 1974), 261.

It is of admirable use to bear the weaknesses, nay, and even the faults, of the real children of God. And the temptations to anger which arise herefrom are often more profitable than any other. Yet surely, for the present, they are not joyous, but grievous: Afterwards comes the peaceable fruit. You shall have exactly as much pain and as much disappointment as will be most for your profit, and just sufficient to

Keep you dead to all below,
Only Christ resolved to know. . . .

Of all gossiping, religious gossiping is the worst: It adds hypocrisy to uncharitableness, and effectually does the work of the devil in the name of the Lord. . . . Let [us] observe, 1. "Now we are to talk of no absent person, but simply of God and our own souls." 2. "The rule of our conversation here is to be the rule of all our conversation. Let us observe it (unless in some necessarily exempt cases) at all times and in all places." If this be frequently inculcated, it will have an excellent effect.

—from a letter to a young disciple, June 20, 1772
The Works of John Wesley, 12:446.

A Prayer of John Wesley:
O Lord, . . . Let me look upon the failings of my neighbour as if

they were my own; that I may be grieved for them, that I may never reveal them but when charity requires . . . Let thy love to me, O blessed Saviour, be the pattern of my love to him. . . . O let me think nothing too dear to part with to set forward the everlasting good of my fellow Christians. . . . AMEN.

—from "A Collection of Forms of Prayer,
for Every Day in the Week"
The Works of John Wesley, 11:210-11.

PERSONAL PRAYER

JOURNAL ENTRY: Reflect on how your love and compassion for others is patterned after Jesus' love for you.

DAY 17

INVOCATION: *Almighty and everlasting God, . . . mercifully this day watch over me with the eyes of thy mercy. Direct my soul and body according to the rule of thy will, and fill my heart with thy Holy Spirit, that I may pass this day, and all the rest of my days, to thy glory. AMEN.*

—from "A Collection of Forms of Prayer,
for Every Day in the Week"
The Works of John Wesley, 11:228.

SCRIPTURE MEDITATION: Eph. 5:1-2

Living a Life of Love

What is that religion, wherewith God is always well pleased? . . .

In a Christian believer *love* sits upon the throne which

is erected in the inmost soul; namely, love of God and man, which fills the whole heart, and reigns without a rival.

In a circle near the throne are all holy tempers;—longsuffering, gentleness, meekness, fidelity, temperance; and if any other were comprised in "the mind which was in Christ Jesus."

In an exterior circle are all the *works of mercy*, whether to the souls or bodies of men. By these we exercise all holy tempers; by these we continually improve them, so that all these are real means of grace, although this is not commonly adverted to.

Next to these are those that are usually termed works of piety;—reading and hearing the word, public, family, private prayer, receiving the Lord's Supper, fasting or abstinence.

Lastly, that his followers may the more effectually provoke one another to love, holy tempers, and good works, our blessed Lord has united them together in one body, the Church, dispersed all over the earth; a little emblem of which, of the Church universal, we have in every particular Christian congregation.

—from Wesley's sermon "On Zeal"
The Works of John Wesley, 7:60-61.

A Prayer of John Wesley:
O God, blessed for ever, we thank and praise thee for all thy benefits, for the comforts of this life, and our hope of everlasting salvation in the life to come. We desire to have a lively sense of thy love always possessing our hearts, that may still constrain us to love thee, to obey thee, to trust in thee, to be content with the portion thy love allots unto us, and to rejoice even in the midst of all the troubles of this life.

Thou hast delivered thine own Son for us all. How shalt thou not with him also freely give us all things? We depend upon thee especially for the grace of thy Holy Spirit. O that we may feel it perpetually bearing us up, by the strength of our most holy faith, above all the temptations that may at any time assault us; that we may keep ourselves unspotted from the world, and may still cleave to thee in righteousness, in lowliness, purity of heart, yea, the whole mind that was in Christ. AMEN.

—from "A Collection of Prayers for Families"
The Works of John Wesley, 11:247.

PERSONAL PRAYER

JOURNAL ENTRY: Take a few moments to diagram the "throne room" Mr. Wesley describes. Does this help you as you "live a life of love" (Eph. 5:2, NIV)?

DAY 18

INVOCATION: *Almighty and everlasting God, . . . mercifully this day watch over me with the eyes of thy mercy. Direct my soul and body according to the rule of thy will, and fill my heart with thy Holy Spirit, that I may pass this day, and all the rest of my days, to thy glory.* AMEN.

—from "A Collection of Forms of Prayer, for Every Day in the Week"
The Works of John Wesley, 11:228.

SCRIPTURE MEDITATION: Eph. 4:17—5:2

A Partaker of Sanctification

You know well that one thing, and one thing only, is needful for you upon earth,—to ensure a better portion, to recover the favour and image of God. The former, by his grace, you have recovered; you have tasted of the love of God. See that you do not cast it away. See that you hold fast the beginning of your confidence steadfast unto the end!

And how soon may you be made a partaker of sanctification! And not only by a slow and insensible growth in grace, but by the power of the Highest overshadowing you, in a moment, in the twinkling of an eye, so as utterly to abolish sin, and to renew you in his whole image! If you are simple of heart, if you are willing to receive the heavenly gift, as a little child, without reasoning, why may you not receive it now? He is nigh that sanctifieth; He is with you; He is knocking at the door of your heart!

>Come in, my Lord, come in,
>And seize her for thine own!

This is the wish of,

My dear friend,
Yours in tender affection,
John Wesley
—from a letter to Miss Cooke, September 24, 1785
The Works of John Wesley, 13:94.

My dear Brother,

As long as you are yourself earnestly aspiring after a full deliverance from all sin, and a renewal in the whole image of God, God will prosper you in your labour; especially if you constantly and strongly exhort all believers to expect full sanctification now, by simple faith. And never be weary of well-doing: In due time you shall reap, if you faint not!

I am
Your affectionate brother,
John Wesley
—letter to Mr. John Ogilvie, August 7, 1785
The Works of John Wesley, 12:527.

A Prayer of John Wesley:
Grant me . . . I beseech thee, O Lord, . . . thy pardon and peace,

that, being cleansed from all my sins, I may serve thee with a quiet mind . . . through Jesus Christ, my Saviour and Redeemer. Amen.
—from "Prayers for Children"
The Works of John Wesley, 11:262.

PERSONAL PRAYER

JOURNAL ENTRY: Reflect a few moments on the importance of being a partaker of sanctification.

DAY 19

INVOCATION: *Almighty and everlasting God, . . . mercifully this day watch over me with the eyes of thy mercy. Direct my soul and body according to the rule of thy will, and fill my heart with thy Holy Spirit, that I may pass this day, and all the rest of my days, to thy glory.* AMEN.
—from "A Collection of Forms of Prayer, for Every Day in the Week"
The Works of John Wesley, 11:228.

SCRIPTURE MEDITATION: Eph. 5:1-14

Christian Character

It is impossible for any that have it, to conceal the religion of Jesus Christ. This our Lord makes plain beyond all contradiction, by a two-fold comparison: "Ye are the light of the world: A city set upon a hill cannot be hid." Ye Christians are "the light of the world," with regard both to your tempers and actions. Your holiness makes you as conspicuous as the sun in the midst of heaven. As ye cannot go out of the world, so neither can ye stay in it without appearing to all mankind. Ye may not flee from men; and while ye are among them, it is impossible to hide your lowliness and meekness, and those other dispositions whereby ye aspire to be perfect as your Father which is in heaven is perfect. Love cannot be hid any more than light; and least of all, when it shines forth in action, when ye exercise yourselves in the labour of love, in beneficence of every kind. As well may men think to hide a city, as to hide a Christian; yea, as well may they conceal a city set upon a hill, as a holy, zealous, active lover of God and man. . . .

So impossible it is, to keep our religion from being seen, unless we cast it away; so vain is the thought of hiding the light, unless by putting it out! Sure it is, that a secret, unobserved religion, cannot be the religion of Jesus Christ. Whatever religion can be concealed, is not Christianity. If a Christian could be hid, he could not be compared to a city set upon a hill; to the light of the world, the sun shining from heaven, and seen by all the world below. Never, therefore, let it enter into the heart of him whom God hath renewed in the spirit of his mind, to hide that light, to keep his religion to himself; especially considering it is not only impossible to conceal true Christianity, but likewise absolutely contrary to the design of the great Author of it.

—from Wesley's sermon "Upon Our Lord's Sermon on the Mount: IV"
The Works of John Wesley, 5:301-2.

Nothing is sin, strictly speaking, but a voluntary transgression of a known law of God. Therefore, every voluntary breach of the law of love is sin; and nothing else, if we speak properly. . . . There may be ten thousand wandering thoughts, and forgetful intervals, without any breach of love . . . Let love fill your heart, and it is enough!

—from a letter to Mrs. Elizabeth Bennis, June 16, 1772
The Works of John Wesley, 12:394.

A Prayer of John Wesley:
We are ashamed, O Lord, to think that ever we have disobeyed thee who hast redeemed us by the precious blood of thine own Son. O that we may agree with thy will in all things for the time to come; and that all the powers of our souls and bodies may be wholly dedicated to thy service. We desire unfeignedly that all the thoughts and designs of our minds, all the affections and tempers of our hearts, and all the actions of our life, may be pure, holy, and unreprovable in thy sight. Amen.
—from "A Collection of Prayers for Families"
The Works of John Wesley, 11:238.

Personal Prayer

Journal Entry: Reflect for a moment on what it means for you to live as a child of the light (see Eph. 5:8).

DAY 20

Invocation: *Almighty and everlasting God, . . . mercifully this day watch over me with the eyes of thy mercy. Direct my soul and body according to the rule of thy will, and fill my heart with thy Holy Spirit, that I may pass this day, and all the rest of my days, to thy glory. Amen.*
—from "A Collection of Forms of Prayer, for Every Day in the Week"
The Works of John Wesley, 11:228.

Scripture Meditation: Eph. 5:15-20

Expecting the Blessing

"I will sprinkle clean water upon you, and ye shall be

clean; from all your filthiness and from all your idols will I cleanse you." "I will circumcise thy heart," (from all sin,) "to love the Lord thy God with all thy heart, and with all thy soul." This I term sanctification, (which is both an instantaneous and a gradual work,) or perfection, the being perfected in love, filled with love . . .

If they like to call this "receiving the Holy Ghost," they may: Only the phrase, in that sense, is not scriptural, and not quite proper; for they all "received the Holy Ghost" when they were justified. God then "sent forth the Spirit of his Son into their hearts, crying, Abba, Father."

O Joseph, keep close to the Bible, both as to sentiment and expression!

—from a letter to Mr. Joseph Benson, December 28, 1770
The Works of John Wesley, 12:416.

"But does God work this great work in the soul gradually or instantaneously?" Perhaps it may be gradually wrought in some; I mean in this sense, they do not advert to the particular moment wherein sin ceases to be. But it is infinitely desirable, were it the will of God, that it should be done instantaneously; that the Lord should destroy sin "by the breath of his mouth," in a moment, in the twinkling of an eye. And so he generally does; a plain fact, of which there is evidence enough to satisfy any unprejudiced person.

Thou therefore look for it every moment! Look for it in the way above described . . . There is then no danger: You can be no worse, if you are no better, for that expectation. For were you to be disappointed of your hope, still you lose nothing. But you shall not be disappointed of your hope: It will come, and will not tarry. Look for it then every day, every hour, every moment! Why not this hour, this moment? Certainly you may look for it *now,* if you believe it is by faith. And by this token you may surely know whether you seek it by faith or by works. If by works, you want something to be done *first, before* you are sanctified.

You think, I must first *be* or *do* thus or thus. Then you are seeking it by works unto this day. If you seek it by faith, you may expect it *as you are;* and if as you are, then expect it *now.* It is of importance to observe, that there is an inseparable connexion between these three points—expect it *by faith,* expect it *as you are,* and expect it *now!* To deny one of them, is to deny them all; to allow one, is to allow them all. Do *you* believe we are sanctified by faith? Be true then to your principle; and look for this blessing just as you are, neither better nor worse; as a poor sinner that has still nothing to pay, nothing to plead, but "Christ *died.*" And if you look for it as you are, then expect it *now.* Stay for nothing: Why should you? Christ is ready; and He is all you want. He is waiting for you: He is at the door! Let your inmost soul cry out, [see prayer below for completion]
  —from Wesley's sermon "The Scripture Way of Salvation"
  The Works of John Wesley, 6:53-54.

A Prayer of John Wesley:
> *Come in, come in, thou heavenly Guest!*
> *Nor hence again remove;*
> *But sup with me, and let the feast*
> *Be everlasting love.*
>
> Amen.
>   —a poem-prayer concluding
>   the sermon quoted above

Personal Prayer

Journal Entry: Take a moment to reflect on what you have just read.

DAY 21

INVOCATION: *Almighty and everlasting God, . . . mercifully this day watch over me with the eyes of thy mercy. Direct my soul and body according to the rule of thy will, and fill my heart with thy Holy Spirit, that I may pass this day, and all the rest of my days, to thy glory.* AMEN.

—from "A Collection of Forms of Prayer, for Every Day in the Week"
The Works of John Wesley, 11:228.

SCRIPTURE MEDITATION: Eph. 5:21-33

Rules for Married Life

My dear Sister,

In the way of life you are entering upon, you will have need of great resolution and steadiness. It will be your wisdom to set out with two rules, and invariably adhere to them.

1. "I will do everything I can to oblige you, except what I cannot do with a clear conscience."

2. "I will refrain from everything I can, that would displease you, except what I cannot refrain from with a clear conscience."

Keep to this, on both sides, from the hour you meet, and your meeting will be a blessing. You will do well likewise, constantly to pray with, as well as for, one another.

Now, Nancy, put on, by the grace of God, the armour of righteousness, on the right hand and on the left! Beware of foolish desires! Beware of inordinate affections! Beware of worldly cares! But, above all, I think, you should beware of wasting time in what is called innocent trifling. And watch against unprofitable conversation, particularly between yourselves. Then your union may be (as it ought) a type of the union between Christ and his church; and you may, in

the end, present each other before Him, holy and unblamable at His coming.
>—letter to Miss Nancy A____, November 2, 1767
>*The Works of John Wesley,* 12:360-61.

A Prayer of John Wesley:
(O most great and mighty Lord,) give to husbands and wives, parents and children, masters and servants, the grace to behave themselves so in their several relations, that they may adorn the doctrine of God our Saviour in all things, and may receive of him a crown of glory; in whose holy name and words we continue to beseech thy grace and mercy towards us and all thy people everywhere, saying, "Our Father," etc. [continue with the Lord's Prayer] . . .
>—from "A Collection of Prayers for Families"
>*The Works of John Wesley,* 11:247.

Personal Prayer

Journal Entry: React to Wesley's rules for married life. How do you see them working in your marriage (or someone else's relationship)?

DAY 22

Invocation: *Fix Thou our steps, O Lord, that we stagger not at the uneven motions of the world, but steadily go on to our glorious home, neither censuring our journey by the weather we meet with nor turning out of the way for anything that befalls us.* Amen.
>—from "A Collection of Forms of Prayer, for Every Day in the Week"
>*Eerdmans' Book of Famous Prayers,* 64.

Scripture Meditation: Eph. 6:1-4

Children

My dear Child,

A Lover of your soul has here drawn a few Prayers, in order to assist you in that great duty. Be sure that you do not omit, at least morning and evening, to present yourself upon your knees before God. You have mercies to pray for, and blessings to praise God for. But take care that you do not mock God, drawing near with your lips, while your heart is far from him. God sees you, and knows your thoughts; therefore, see that you not only speak with your lips, but pray with your heart. And that you may not ask in vain, see that you forsake sin, and make it your endeavour to do what God has shown you ought; because God says, "The prayers of the wicked are an abomination unto the Lord." Ask then of God for the blessings you want, in the name, and for the sake, of Jesus Christ; and God will hear and answer you, and do more for you than you can either ask or think.

John Wesley
—from the Preface of "Prayers for Children"
The Works of John Wesley, 11:259.

But what is implied in, "Children, obey your parents in all things?" Certainly the First point of obedience is to do nothing which your father or mother forbids, whether it be great or small. Nothing is more plain, than that the prohibition of a parent binds every conscientious child; that is, except the thing prohibited is clearly enjoined of God. . . .

The Second thing implied in this direction is, Do every thing which your father or mother bids, be it great or small, provided it be not contrary to any command of God. . . .

It is with admirable wisdom that the Father of spirits has given this direction, that as the strength of the parents supplies the want of strength, and the understanding of the parents the want of understanding, in their children, till they have strength and understanding of their own; so the will of the parents may guide that of their children till they have wisdom and experience to guide themselves. This, therefore, is the very first thing which children have to learn,—that they are to obey their parents, to submit to their will, in all things . . .

Accordingly, St. Paul directs all parents to bring up their children "in the discipline and doctrine of the Lord." For their will may be broken by proper discipline, even in their early infancy; whereas it must be a considerable time after, before they are capable of instruction. This, therefore, is the first point of all: Bow down their wills from the very first dawn of reason; and, by habituating them to your will, prepare them for submitting to the will of their Father which is in heaven.

—from Wesley's sermon "On Obedience to Parents"
The Works of John Wesley, 7:101-2.

A PRAYER OF JOHN WESLEY:
O thou blessed Guide of my youth, give me thy grace to seek after thee in my early years, that thou mayest not be unmindful of me in the time of age. . . . Amen.

—from "Prayers for Children"
The Works of John Wesley, 11:271-72.

PERSONAL PRAYER

JOURNAL ENTRY: Reflect on the fact that Mr. Wesley had no children of his own. How practical is his advice?

DAY 23

INVOCATION: *Fix Thou our steps, O Lord, that we stagger not at the uneven motions of the world, but steadily go on to our glorious*

home, neither censuring our journey by the weather we meet with nor turning out of the way for anything that befalls us. AMEN.
—from "A Collection of Forms of Prayer, for Every Day in the Week"
Eerdmans' Book of Famous Prayers, 64.

SCRIPTURE MEDITATION: Eph. 6:5-9

Honest Industry

Gain all you can by honest industry. Use all possible diligence in your calling. Lose no time. If you understand yourself, and your relation to God and man, you know you have none to spare. If you understand your particular calling, as you ought, you will have no time that hangs upon your hands. Every business will afford some employment sufficient for every day and every hour. That wherein you are placed, if you follow it in earnest, will leave you no leisure for silly, unprofitable diversions. You have always something better to do, something that will profit you, more or less. And "whatsoever thy hand findeth to do, do it with thy might." Do it as soon as possible: No delay! No putting off from day to day, or from hour to hour! Never leave anything till to-morrow, which you can do to-day. And do it as well as possible. Do not sleep or yawn over it: Put your whole strength to the work. Spare no pains. Let nothing be done by halves, or in a slight and careless manner. Let nothing in your business be left undone, if it can be done by labour or patience.

Gain all you can, by common sense, by using in your business all the understanding which God has given you. It is amazing to observe, how few do this; how men run on in the same dull track with their forefathers. But whatever they do who know not God, this is no rule for you. It is a shame for a Christian not to improve upon *them*, in whatever he takes in hand. You should be continually learning, from the experience of others, or from your own experience, reading, and reflection, to do everything you have to do better to-day than you did yesterday. And see that you practise whatever you learn, that you may make the best of all that is in your hands.

—from Wesley's sermon "The Use of Money"
The Works of John Wesley, 6:130.

Dear Sir,

. . . I find the engaging, though but a little, in these temporal affairs, is apt to damp and deaden the soul; and there is no remedy, but continual prayer. What, then, but the mighty power of God can keep your soul alive, who are engaged all the day long with such a multiplicity of them? It is well that his grace is sufficient for you. But do you not find need to pray always? And if you cannot always say,—

"My hands are but employed below,
My heart is still with thee;"

is there not the more occasion for some season of solemn retirement, (if it were possible, every day,) wherein you may withdraw your mind from earth, and even the accounts between God and your own soul? I commend you and yours to His continual protection . . .

—from a letter to Mr. Wesley's banker, Mr. Blackwell, March 15, 1747-48
The Works of John Wesley, 12:169-70.

A Prayer of John Wesley:
Deliver me, O God, from too intense an application to even necessary business. . . . I know the narrowness of my heart, and that an eager attention to earthly things leaves it no room for the things of heaven. O teach me to go through all my employments with so truly disengaged a heart, that I may still see thee in all things. Amen.

—from "A Collection of Forms of Prayer, For Every Day in the Week"
The Works of John Wesley, 11:207.

PERSONAL PRAYER

JOURNAL ENTRY: Reflect on how you balance a strong work ethic and a strong desire to be a man or woman of God.

DAY 24

INVOCATION: *Fix Thou our steps, O Lord, that we stagger not at the uneven motions of the world, but steadily go on to our glorious home, neither censuring our journey by the weather we meet with nor turning out of the way for anything that befalls us.* AMEN.
—from "A Collection of Forms of Prayer, for Every Day in the Week"
Eerdmans' Book of Famous Prayers, 64.

SCRIPTURE MEDITATION: Eph. 6:10-12

Satan's Devices, Part 1

The devices whereby the subtle god of this world labours to destroy the children of God—or at least to torment whom he cannot destroy, to perplex and hinder them in running the race which is set before them—are numberless as the stars of heaven, or the sand upon the sea-shore. But it is of one of them only that I now propose to speak . . .

The inward kingdom of heaven, which is set up in the hearts of all that repent and believe the gospel, is no other than "righteousness, and peace, and joy in the Holy Ghost." Every babe in Christ knows we are made partakers of these, the very hour that we believe in Jesus. But these are only the firstfruits of his Spirit; the harvest is not yet. Although these blessings are inconceivably great, yet we trust to see greater than these. We trust to love the Lord our God, not only as we do now, with a weak, though sincere affection, but "with all our heart, with all our mind, with all our soul, and with all our strength." We look for power to "rejoice evermore, to pray without ceasing, and in every thing to give thanks;" knowing, "this is the will of God in Christ Jesus concerning us."

We expect to be "made perfect in love;" in that which casts out all painful fear, and all desire but that of glorifying him we love, and of loving and serving him more and more....

Now this is the grand device of Satan, to destroy the first work of God in the soul, or at least to hinder its increase, by our expectation of that greater work....

... He endeavours to damp our joy in the Lord, by the consideration of our own vileness, sinfulness, unworthiness ... So that we cannot rejoice in what we have, because there is more which we have not.... Likewise, the deeper conviction God works in us of our present unholiness, and the more vehement desire we feel in our heart of the entire holiness he hath promised, the more are we tempted to think lightly of the present gifts of God, and to undervalue what we have already received, because of what we have not received....

You may cast back this dart upon [Satan's] own head, while, through the grace of God, the more you feel of your own vileness, the more you rejoice in confident hope, that all this shall be done away. While you hold fast this hope, every evil temper you feel, though you hate it with a perfect hatred, may be a means, not of lessening your humble joy, but rather of increasing it.... By this means, the greater that change is which remains to be wrought in your soul, the more may you triumph in the Lord, and rejoice in the God of your salvation, who hath done so great things for you already, and will do so much greater things than these.

—from Wesley's sermon "Satan's Devices"

The Works of John Wesley, 6:32-34, 39-40.

A Prayer of John Wesley:
I desire to offer unto thee, O Lord, my evening [or morning] sacrifice of praise and thanksgiving for all thy mercies bestowed upon me. I bless thee for my creation, preservation, and, above all, for my redemption by our Lord and Saviour Jesus Christ. . . . Amen.

—from "Prayers for Children"
The Works of John Wesley, 11:271-72.

Personal Prayer

Journal Entry: Reflect on times when Satan has tried to rob you of your joy by undervaluing what you have received when compared to what you still have need to receive.

DAY 25

Invocation: *Fix Thou our steps, O Lord, that we stagger not at the uneven motions of the world, but steadily go on to our glorious home, neither censuring our journey by the weather we meet with nor turning out of the way for anything that befalls us.* Amen.

—from "A Collection of Forms of Prayer, for Every Day in the Week"
Eerdmans' Book of Famous Prayers, 64.

Scripture Meditation: Eph. 6:10-17

Satan's Devices, Part 2

If [Satan] can damp our joy, he will soon attack our peace also. He will suggest, "Are you fit to see God? He is of purer eyes than to behold iniquity. How, then, can you flatter yourself, so as to imagine he beholds you with approbation? God is holy: You are unholy. What communion hath light with darkness? How is it possible that you, unclean as you are, should be in a state of acceptance with God? . . . How can you presume . . . to think that all your sins are already blotted out? How can this be, until you are brought nearer to God, until you bear more resemblance to him?" Thus will he endeavour not only to shake your peace, but even to overturn the very foundation of it; to bring you back . . . to the point from whence you set out first, even to seek for justification by works, or by your own righteousness . . .

The more vehemently he assaults your peace with that suggestion . . . take the more earnest heed to hold fast that, "Not by works of righteousness which I had done, I am found in him; I am accepted in the Beloved; not having my own righteousness . . . but that which is by faith in Christ, the righteousness which is of God by faith." O bind this about your neck: Write it upon the table of thy heart. Wear it as a bracelet upon thy arm, as frontlets between thine eyes: "I am 'justified freely by his grace, through the redemption that is in Jesus Christ.'" Value and esteem, more and more, that precious truth, "By grace we are saved through faith." Admire, more and more, the free grace of God, in so loving the world as to give "his only begotten Son, that whosoever believeth on him might not perish, but have everlasting life." So shall the sense of the sinfulness you feel, on the one hand, and of the holiness you expect, on the other, both contribute to establish your peace, and to make it flow as a river. So shall that peace flow on with an even stream, in spite of all those mountains of ungodliness, which shall become a plain in the day when the Lord cometh to take full possession of your heart.

—from Wesley's sermon "Satan's Devices"

The Works of John Wesley, 6:34, 40.

A Prayer of John Wesley:
I know, O Lord, that thou hast commanded me, and therefore it is my duty, to love thee with all my heart, and with all my strength. I know thou art infinitely holy and overflowing in all perfection; and therefore it is my duty so to love thee.

I know thou hast created me, and that I have neither being nor blessing but what is the effect of thy power and goodness.

I know thou art the end for which I was created, and that I can expect no happiness but in thee.

I know that in love to me, being lost in sin, thou didst send thy only Son, and that he, being the Lord of glory, did humble himself to the death upon the cross, that I might be raised to glory.

I know thou hast provided me with all necessary helps for carrying me through this life to that eternal glory, and this out of the excess of thy pure mercy to me, unworthy of all mercies.

I know thou hast promised to be thyself my "exceeding great reward;" though it is thou alone who thyself "workest in me, both to will and to do of thy good pleasure."

Upon these, and many other titles, I confess it is my duty to love thee, my God, with all my heart. Amen.

—from "A Collection of Forms of Prayer, for Every Day in the Week"
The Works of John Wesley, 11:204.

Personal Prayer

Journal Entry: Has Satan ever tried to rob you of your peace in the way Mr. Wesley has suggested?

DAY 26

Invocation: *Fix Thou our steps, O Lord, that we stagger not at the uneven motions of the world, but steadily go on to our glorious*

home, neither censuring our journey by the weather we meet with nor turning out of the way for anything that befalls us. AMEN.
—from "A Collection of Forms of Prayer, for Every Day in the Week"
Eerdmans' Book of Famous Prayers, 64.

SCRIPTURE MEDITATION: Eph. 6:10-17

The Armour of God

First, as a general preservative against all the rage, the power, and subtlety of your great adversary, put on the panoply, "the whole armour of God," universal holiness. See that "the mind be in you which was also in Christ Jesus," and that ye "walk as Christ also walked;" that ye have a "conscience void of offence toward God and toward men." So shall ye be "able to withstand" all the force and all the stratagems of the enemy: So shall ye be able to "withstand in the evil day," in the day of sore temptation, and "having done all to stand," to remain in the posture of victory and triumph.

To his "fiery darts,"—his evil suggestions of every kind, blasphemous or unclean, though numberless as the stars of heaven,—oppose the "shield of faith." A consciousness of the love of Christ Jesus will effectually quench them all.

Jesus hath died for *you!*
What can your faith withstand?
Believe, hold fast your shield! and who
Shall pluck you from his hand?

If he injects doubts whether you are a child of God, or fears lest you should not endure to the end; "take to you for a helmet the hope of salvation." Hold fast that glad word, "Blessed be the God and Father of our Lord Jesus Christ, who, according to his abundant mercy, hath begotten us again unto a living hope of an inheritance incorruptible, undefiled, and that fadeth not away." You will never be overthrown, you will never be staggered by your adversary . . .

Whenever the "roaring lion, walking about and seeking whom he may devour," assaults you with all his malice, and rage, and strength, "resist" him "steadfast in the faith." Then is the time, having cried to the Strong for strength, to "stir up the gift of God that is in you;" to summon all your faith, and hope, and love; to turn the attack in the name of the Lord, and in the power of his might; and "he will" soon "flee from you."

But "there is no temptation," says one, "greater than the being without temptation." When, therefore, this is the case, when Satan seems to be withdrawn, then beware lest he hurt you more as a crooked serpent, than he could do as a roaring lion. Then take care you are not lulled into a pleasing slumber; lest he ... draw you ... from seeking all your happiness in Him.

Lastly. If he "transform himself into an angel of light," then are you in the greatest danger of all. Then have you need to beware, lest you also fall, where many mightier have been slain; then have you the greatest need to "watch and pray, that ye enter not into temptation."

—from Wesley's sermon "Of Evil Angels"
The Works of John Wesley, 6:379-80.

A PRAYER OF JOHN WESLEY:
O Saviour of the world, God of Gods, light of light, thou that art the brightness of thy Father's glory, the express image of his person; thou that hast destroyed the power of the devil, that hast overcome death, "that sittest at the right hand of the Father;" thou wilt speedily come down in thy Father's glory to judge all men according to their works: Be thou my light and my peace; destroy the power of the devil in me, and make me a new creature. AMEN.

—from "A Collection of Forms of Prayer, for Every Day in the Week"
The Works of John Wesley, 11:228.

PERSONAL PRAYER

JOURNAL ENTRY: Meditate on and react to the statement "There is no temptation greater than the being without temptation."

DAY 27

INVOCATION: *Fix Thou our steps, O Lord, that we stagger not at the uneven motions of the world, but steadily go on to our glorious home, neither censuring our journey by the weather we meet with nor turning out of the way for anything that befalls us.* AMEN.

—from "A Collection of Forms of Prayer, for Every Day in the Week"
Eerdmans' Book of Famous Prayers, 64.

SCRIPTURE MEDITATION: Eph. 6:18-20

Forms of Prayer

Although there may be some use in teaching very young children to "say their prayers daily;" yet I judge it to be utterly impossible to teach any to "practise prayer," till they are awakened. For, what is prayer, but the desire of the soul expressed in words to God, either inwardly or outwardly? How then will you teach them to express a desire who feel no desire at all?

—from a letter to a young disciple, September 8, 1773
The Works of John Wesley, 12:450.

By our reading prayers we prevent our people's contracting an hatred for forms of prayer; which would naturally be the case, if we always prayed extempore.

—from a letter to Mr. William Percival, February 17, 1787
The Works of John Wesley, 13:113.

The generality of Christians, as soon as they rise, are accustomed to use some kind of *prayer;* and probably to use the same form still, which they learned when they are eight or ten years old. Now, I do not condemn those who proceed thus, (though many do,) as mocking God; though they have used the same form, without any variation, for twenty or thirty years together. But surely there is "a more excellent way" of ordering our private devotions. What if you were to follow the advice given by that great and good man, Mr. Law, on this subject? Consider both your outward and inward state, and vary your prayers accordingly. . . . pour out your soul before God in such prayer as is suited to your circumstances. . . . You may, likewise, when you have time, add to your other devotions a little reading and meditation, and perhaps a psalm of praise,—the natural effusion of a thankful heart. You must certainly see, that this is "a more excellent way" than the poor dry form which you used before.

—from Wesley's sermon "The More Excellent Way"
The Works of John Wesley, 7:30.

A Prayer of John Wesley:
Fix thou our steps, O Lord, that we stagger not at the uneven motions of the world, but steadily go on to our glorious home, neither censuring our journey by the weather we meet with nor turning out of the way for anything that befalls us.

The winds are often rough, and our own weight presses us downwards. Reach forth, O Lord, thy hand, thy saving hand, and speedily deliver us.

Teach us, O Lord, to use this transitory life as pilgrims returning to their beloved home; that we may take what our journey requires, and not think of settling in a foreign country.
Amen.

—from "A Collection of Forms of Prayer, for Every Day in the Week"
Eerdmans' Book of Famous Prayers, 64.

PERSONAL PRAYER

JOURNAL ENTRY: By "forms of prayer" Mr. Wesley meant written or memorized prayers. Reflect on the value of using a form of prayer as well as extemporaneous prayer.

DAY 28

INVOCATION: *Fix Thou our steps, O Lord, that we stagger not at the uneven motions of the world, but steadily go on to our glorious home, neither censuring our journey by the weather we meet with nor turning out of the way for anything that befalls us. AMEN.*

—from "A Collection of Forms of Prayer, for Every Day in the Week"
Eerdmans' Book of Famous Prayers, 64.

SCRIPTURE MEDITATION: Eph. 6:21-24

Self-examination

PARTICULAR QUESTIONS RELATIVE TO THE LOVE OF GOD [for Sunday Evening]

1. Have I set apart some of this day to think upon his perfections and mercies?
2. Have I laboured to make this day a day of heavenly rest, sacred to divine love?
3. Have I employed those parts of it in works of necessity and mercy, which were not employed in prayer, reading, and meditation?

GENERAL QUESTIONS, WHICH MAY BE USED EVERY MORNING

1. Did I think of God first and last?

2. Have I examined myself how I behaved since last night's retirement?

3. Am I resolved to do all the good I can this day, and to be diligent in the business of my calling?

PARTICULAR QUESTIONS RELATING TO THE LOVE OF OUR NEIGHBOUR

1. Have I thought anything but my conscience too dear to part with, to please or serve my neighbour?

2. Have I rejoiced or grieved with him?

3. Have I received his infirmities with pity, not with anger?

4. Have I contradicted any one, either where I had no good end in view, or where there was no probability of convincing?

5. Have I let him I thought in the wrong (in a trifle) have the last word?

—from "A Collection of Forms of Prayer, for Every Day in the Week"
The Works of John Wesley, 11:206-7, 209, 211-12.

A PRAYER OF JOHN WESLEY:
O thou, my adored Redeemer, be thou the wish of my heart, the scope and end of all my time.

Soon as I awake, let me look up to thee; and when I arise, first lowly bow to thee.

Often in the day let me call in my thoughts to thee; and when I go to rest, close up mine eyes in thee.

So shall my time be governed by thy grace and my eternity crowned with thy glory. AMEN.

John Wesley's Prayers, 109.

PERSONAL PRAYER

JOURNAL ENTRY: What is your reaction to these questions for self-examination?

DAY 29

INVOCATION: *Kindle in our hearts, O Lord, thy holy fire, that we may offer to thee the incense of praise.* AMEN.
—from "The Office of the Holy Ghost"
John Wesley's Prayers, 109.

SCRIPTURE MEDITATION: Eph. 5:1-2

Favorite Quotations from the Letters of John Wesley, Part 1

(The following are some of my favorite lines from John Wesley's correspondence.)

You may lose this sense [of God's love] either, 1. By committing sin. Or, 2. By omitting duty. Or, 3. By giving way to pride, anger, or any other inward sin. Or, 4. By not watching unto prayer; by yielding to indolence, or spiritual sloth. But it is no more necessary that we should ever lose it, than it is necessary we should omit duty or commit sin.
—from a letter to Miss Furly, May 18, 1757
The Works of John Wesley, 12:197.

There may be some rare cases wherein God has determined not to bestow his perfect love till a little before death; but this I believe is uncommon: He does not usually put off the fulfilling of his promises. Seek, and you shall find; seek earnestly, and you shall find speedily.
—from a letter to the same, September 6, 1757
The Works of John Wesley, 12:200.

It matters not how long we live, but how well.
—from a letter to the same, June 1, 1760
The Works of John Wesley, 12:206.

But these souls dwell in a shattered, corruptible body, and are so pressed down thereby, that they cannot exert their love as they would, by always thinking, speaking, and acting precisely right. For want of better bodily or-

gans, they sometimes inevitably think, speak, or act wrong. Yet I think they need the advocacy of Christ, even for these involuntary defects; although they do not imply a defect of love, but of understanding.
>—from a letter to Miss Elizabeth Hardy, December 26, 1761
>*The Works of John Wesley*, 12:236.

Always remember, the essence of Christian holiness is simplicity and purity; one design, one desire; entire devotion to God.
>—from a letter to a member of the society, April 14, 1771
>*The Works of John Wesley*, 12:289.

But beware you be not swallowed up in books: An ounce of love is worth a pound of knowledge.
>—from a letter to Mr. Joseph Benson, November 7, 1768
>*The Works of John Wesley*, 12:409.

If we could once bring all . . . uniformly and steadily to insist on those two points, "Christ dying for us," and "Christ reigning in us," we should shake the trembling gates of hell.
>—from a letter to Mr. Charles Perronet, December 28, 1774
>*The Works of John Wesley*, 12:460.

Sanctified crosses are blessings indeed; and when it is best, our Lord will remove them.
>—from a letter to Miss Mary Stokes, December 26, 1771
>*The Works of John Wesley*, 12:516.

A Prayer of John Wesley:
Be thou with me, O Lord, this day, to bless and keep, guide and govern me, and let me be thine, and only thine, for ever. Amen.
>—*The Works of John Wesley*, 11:269.

Personal Prayer

Journal Entry: Reflect on one quotation from those above.

DAY 30

INVOCATION: *Kindle in our hearts, O Lord, thy holy fire, that we may offer to thee the incense of praise.* AMEN.
—from "The Office of the Holy Ghost"
John Wesley's Prayers, 109.

SCRIPTURE MEDITATION: Eph. 3:14-21

Favorite Quotations, Part 2

Trials are only blessings in disguise.
—from a letter to Mr. Zechariah Yewdall, July 24, 1780
The Works of John Wesley, 13:10.

We have but one point in view; to be altogether Christians, scriptural, rational Christians. For which we well know, not only the world, but the almost Christians, will never forgive us.
—from a letter to Miss Bishop, 1767
The Works of John Wesley, 13:17.

Remember the wise saying of Mr. Dodd, "It is a great loss to lose an affliction." If you are no better for it, you lose it. But you may gain thereby both humility, seriousness, and resignation.
—from a letter to the same, June 17, 1774
The Works of John Wesley, 13:27.

It is a true saying, "The soul and the body make the man; and the spirit and discipline make a Christian."
—from a letter to Mr. Adam Clarke, January 3, 1787
The Works of John Wesley, 13:101.

Mr. Hoskins . . . asked the favour of your Lordship to ordain him, that he might minister to a little flock in America. But your Lordship did not see good to ordain him: But your Lordship did see good to ordain, and send into America, other persons, who knew something of Greek and

Latin; but who knew no more of saving souls, than of catching whales.

> —from a letter to Bishop Lowth, August 10, 1780
> *The Works of John Wesley,* 13:143.

O make haste. Be a Christian, a real Bible Christian now! You may say, "Nay, I am a Christian already." I fear not. (See how freely I speak.) A Christian is not afraid to die. Are not you? Do you desire to depart, and to be with Christ? . . . O let your heart cry to Him, "What I know not teach thou me. Let me not die before I long to die! Give me the wisdom that sitteth by thy throne, and reject me not from among thy children!"

> —from a letter to Miss C____, June 8, 1773
> *The Works of John Wesley,* 13:68-69.

We must, we must, you and I at least, be all devoted to God! . . . Let us this day use all the power we have! If we have enough, well; if not, let us this day expect a fresh supply. How long shall we drag on thus heavily, though God has called us to be the chief conductors of such a work? Alas! What conductors! If I am (in some sense) the head, and you the heart, of the work; may it not be said, "The whole head is sick, and the whole heart is faint?" Come, in the name of God, let us arise, and shake ourselves from the dust! Let us strengthen each other's hands in God, and that without delay.

> —from a letter to John's brother Charles Wesley, February 28, 1766
> *The Works of John Wesley,* 12:129-30.

O what a thing it is to have *curam animarum* (the care of souls)! You and I are called to this; to save souls from death; to watch over them as those that must give account! If our office implied no more than preaching a few times in a week, I could play with it: So might you. But how small a part of our duty (yours as well as mine) is this! God says to you, as well as me, "Do all thou canst, be it more or less, to save the souls for whom my Son has died." Let this voice be ever sounding in our ears; then shall we give up our account with joy. *Eia age, rumpe moras* (Come, bestir yourself, and lay aside delay)! I am ashamed of my indolence and inactivity. The good Lord help us both! Adieu!

—from a letter to the same, March 25, 1772
The Works of John Wesley, 12:138.

A Prayer of John Wesley:
What I know not teach thou me. Let me not die before I long to die! Give me the wisdom that sitteth by thy throne, and reject me not from among thy children! Amen.

The Works of John Wesley, 13:68-69.

Personal Prayer

Journal Entry: Which of these quotations strikes a chord in you?

WORKS CITED

The Book of Worship for Church and Home. Nashville: Methodist Publishing House, 1964.

Demaray, Donald E., ed. *Devotions and Prayers of John Wesley.* Grand Rapids: Baker Book House, 1957.

Gill, Frederick C., ed. *John Wesley's Prayers.* New York: Abingdon-Cokesbury Press, 1951.

Telford, John, ed. *The Letters of the Rev. John Wesley, A.M.* 8 vols. London: Epworth Press, 1960.

Wesley, John. *The Works of John Wesley.* 3rd ed. 14 vols. Kansas City: Beacon Hill Press of Kansas City, 1978-79 reprint of 1872 edition.

Wirt, Sherwood Eliot, and Kersten Beckstrom, ed. *Living Quotations for Christians.* New York: Harper and Row, 1974.

Zundell, Veronica, comp. *Eerdmans' Book of Famous Prayers.* Grand Rapids: William B. Eerdmans Publishing Co., reprinted 1985.